Young People's
SCIENCE
Encyclopedia

Index by Sara Lamb

Edited by the Staff of

NATIONAL COLLEGE OF EDUCATION

Evanston, Illinois

Volume 20
Index

P.O. Box 1229
Antioch, California 94509

Photographs

Page 2: Skylab space station (NASA)

Page 3: *Top to Bottom:*
Wheatfield (U.S.D.A. Photo)
Technician capping Abbokinase (Abbott Laboratories)
Spider (Macmillan Science Company)
View of Earth (NASA)
Space Shuttle (NASA)
Bahama coral reef (Macmillan Science Company)

Cover: Design by Sandra Gelak
Wheat Harvester (USDA Photo)
Wood Duck (James P. Rowan)
Walking Stick (James P. Rowan)

Library of Congress Catalog Card Number: 67-17925

4 5 6 7 8 9 10 11 12 R 85 84 83 82

TABLE OF CONTENTS

YOUNG PEOPLE'S
SCIENCE ENCYCLOPEDIA

Edited by the Staff of
NATIONAL COLLEGE OF EDUCATION, Evanston, Illinois

ASSOCIATE EDITORS

HELEN J. CHALLAND, B.E., M.A., Ph.D.
  Chairman, Division of Natural Sciences
  National College of Education,
  Evanston, Illinois

DONALD A. BOYER, B.S., M.S., Ph.D.
  Science Education Consultant, Winnetka
  Public Schools, Winnetka, Illinois
  Science, National College of Education

EDITORIAL CONSULTANTS
ON THE STAFF OF NATIONAL COLLEGE OF EDUCATION

Elizabeth R. Brandt, B.A., M.Ed.
Eugene B. Cantelupe, B.A., M.F.A., Ph.D.
John H. Daugherty, B.S., M.A.
Irwin K. Feinstein, B.S., M.A., Ph.D.
Mary Gallagher, A.B., M.A., Ph.D.
Beatrice S. Garber, A.B., M.S., Ph.D.
Hal S. Galbreath, B.S. Ed., M.S.
Arthur J. Hannah, B.S., M.Ed., Ed.D.

Robert R. Kidder, A.B., M.A., Ph.D.
Jean C. Kraft, B.S., M.A., Ph.D.
Elise P. Lerman, B.A., B.F.A., M.F.A.
Mary M. Lindquist, B.A., M.A., Ph.D.
Mary-Louise Neumann, A.B., B.S.L.S.
Lavon Rasco, B.A., M.A., Ph.D.
Bruce Allen Thale, B.S.Ed., M.S.Ed.
Fred R.Wilkins, Jr., B.A., M.Ed., Ph.D.

SPECIAL SUBJECT AREA CONSULTANTS

Krafft A. Ehricke, B.A.E., H.L.D.
Benjamin M. Hair, A.B., M.D.
Charles B. Johnson, B.S., M.A., M.S.
Raymond J. Johnson, B.B.A., M.Ed.

H. Kenneth Scatliff, M.D.
Eleanor S. Segal, M.D.
Paul P. Sipiera, B.A., M.S.
Ray C. Soliday, B.A., B.S., M.A. (Deceased)

Don Dwiggins, Aviation Editor

THE STAFF

Project Director   Rudolph A. Hastedt
Project Editor   M. Frances Dyra
Editorial Assistant   Janet Zelasko

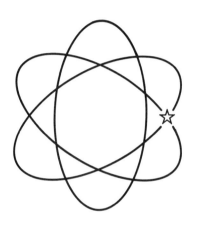

Helping Young People in Science

A message for parents and teachers . . .

Science holds more interest for more young people today than any other field of knowledge. Most parents and teachers know that motivating children to study science is hardly necessary. Not only are the things of science, such as animals, plants, astronauts, spaceships, and rocks, of interest to young people; but their natural curiosity, their tendency to question, and their habit of testing everything exemplify the ways of the scientist. Unfortunately, many children tend to lose these characteristics as they grow to maturity. Parents and teachers can help to keep them alive and vibrant by careful guidance.

Science should be an integral part of our way of life. Its processes have much to offer society and the development of personality. Increasingly and surely, science is taking the center of the stage in modern civilization, and will pervade the existence and critically affect the lives of today's children in ways the present generation cannot even imagine. Parents and teachers have an obligation to guide the learning of the rising generation so that scientific technology does not become the enslaver but the enslaved. Through the study of science men can free their minds of fear, superstition, prejudice, and ignorance. Through it men can learn a new way of thinking and a saner way of deliberating, as well as acquire a greater respect for law and order and a new chance for the development of democracy. Science can be used, however, to destroy the freedom of the mind and the freedom of the peoples. The way by which science is taught — or the way children learn it — is the key to their future.

Whether the children of today will bend technology toward the building of a happier, safer world tomorrow depends, in part, on the expectations held by parents and teachers. If they care enough about education, about honest and objective inquiry, about deliberative rather than impulsive action, and about the fulfillment of the human individual to his optimum, much of the present generation's responsibility will have been discharged.

Obviously, *example* is the best way to show expectation. Parents who provide good books in the home for their children but never open books themselves fail to inspire the child to learn. It is a good intellectual climate for a child when lively discussions and questions in the family circle lead to dictionaries, encyclopedic volumes, or other source materials which throw light on the puzzling and the unknown. The habit of such family deliberation which depends on the "look it up" technique rather than on the lazy exchange of ignorance could change significantly the direction of human affairs. It will surely improve the school achievement and the intellectual and social growth of children.

It is the obligation of every parent and teacher to help each child achieve as much as his powers permit. Excellence in education cannot be restricted to the intellectual elite in a society where enterprises are so complex as ours. All types of people are needed to perform to the maximum if the success of the whole is to be ensured. On this problem, John W. Gardner[1], President of the Carnegie Foundation, says that excellence of performance in launching a rocket missile is required of each person who has anything to do with it from the time it is designed on the drawing boards until the last minute when a mechanic adjusts the final valve

[1] John W. Gardner, *Excellence* (New York: Harper & Brothers, 1961) p. 131.

before it is blasted from its pad. A mistake anywhere along the line of production or of the launching operation could cause the rocket to blow up with a great waste of time, money, and even of human life. Therefore, it is in the interest of national survival that parents and teachers help every child to make steady progress in his education at his own best level or rate of performance.

Adequate materials which can be adapted to individual differences in ability and interest should become the possession of every home and every classroom. The encyclopedia is by far the most versatile of the source materials available. Not only is it a depository of a greater fund of information but it is, by its inherent organization, more efficient to use because of its pinpointing of individual entries arranged in alphabetical order. When the articles, such as those of the YOUNG PEOPLE'S SCIENCE ENCYCLOPEDIA, are written for a wide range of ability, the possibility is enhanced that every child may find something of value to him at his level of achievement. In the home, children of varying ages may profit from the use of such a treasury of knowledge and easy-to-do experiments.

What is science? A scientist?

Science primarily is a voyage of discovery, and a working scientist is a person in pursuit of the unknown. The pursuit is aided by increasingly better instruments, tools, and ways of thinking. To build up knowledge and to improve man's grasp or understanding of his universe home — from its very big aspects to the very little — is the aim of science.

The YOUNG PEOPLE'S SCIENCE ENCYCLOPEDIA gives to the teacher or the parent an unmatched opportunity to guide the child in using valuable information, experiments, and cross references to solve problems, to build attitudes, and to develop ways of thinking like those of the mature scientist. Let it be understood, however, that scientific thinking is not confined to scientists. The encyclopedia can be used to build the foundation for careers other than in science. All scholars, statesmen, and philosophers who achieve greatness govern their activities by such scientific attitudes and ways of thinking as:

1. Honesty in reporting about events or data
2. Maintaining healthy skepticism toward apparent facts
3. Refusing to jump to quick conclusions but preferring to hear all sides and collect all available evidence
4. Accepting the probability of change

5. Open-mindedness toward new ideas
6. Searching constantly for mistakes and omissions in one's own work
7. Cheerfully admitting one's own mistakes
8. Accepting the obligation to test one's own conclusions and to encourage others to test them.

Such attitudes or ways of thinking, which are implicit in the study of science, help to develop better personal character among today's children and youth. If science can become the partner of democracy, its effect on citizenship ultimately should contribute to a better society.

What do young people learn in science before high school? The contents of a boy's pockets or the treasure chest under his bed can give significant leads. Perhaps there are bird's eggs, a sling shot, a telescope, some rock quartz, and a pressed leaf. To the mature scientist these things can represent some of the main areas of knowledge in science: zoology, physics, astronomy, geology, and botany, respectively. But science for young people does not deal in the technical material and vocabulary of such advanced fields of science. It begins simply with something like the bird's eggs and takes the young person through a study of the familiar living things around him to the distant and the microscopic. When he reaches his first course in biology at the high school level, he is on much familiar ground.

Since science is taught in every grade level of the elementary and junior high schools, it is important for the parent as well as for the teacher to know how broadly it is based on the total content of all the sciences. In an elementary way the student is given a picture of the whole. He gets a general view of the entire universe from the extremely tiny animal under the microscope to the largest galaxy or system of stars. He is not expected to study in depth at this age, although intellectually gifted students may be encouraged to go deeper if their interest is high and other curriculum areas are not neglected. This broad picture of science as the young person views it in school has these main subdivisions:

I. The earth and its crust
   A. Rocks, minerals, and soils
   B. Erosion by wind, water, gravity, frost, and glacial action
   C. Mountain-building
   D. Earthquakes and volcanoes
   E. The continents and the seas
   F. Other land forms
II. Beyond the earth

        A. Atmosphere and weather
        B. Space
        C. Planets, stars, and galaxies
        D. Satellites: moons and man-made
        E. Air and space travel
    III.   Living things
        A. Plants
        B. Animals
        C. Health and physiology
    IV.   Energies and physical-chemical forces
        A. Light and color
        B. Sound
        C. Electricity and magnetism
        D. Combustion and heat
        E. Air and other gas pressures
        F. Water power
        G. Mechanics
        H. Gravity
        I. Nuclear fission and fusion
        J. Chemical change
        K. Physical change
    V.   Inventions, discoveries, and great men of science

The method of discovery

One of the basic needs of children is new experiences which expand their knowledge of the world about them. They show this need constantly by the questions they ask. Their desire to explore is insatiable, as every father and mother can testify. The method of discovery is based on this need, and guides the explorations of young people so that they learn significantly from their activities of discovery.

The boy or girl whose study of science is a voyage of discovery rather than a passive absorption of content is himself a young scientist. Leaders in the academic world today are emphasizing the value of a student's learning a field of knowledge precisely the way in which the experts of that field develop and expand its facts and principles.[2] In almost every field, content is developed through research and less formal processes of discovery which reflect the attitudes and methods of the scientists. Even though knowledge in a field is known to mature scholars, teachers and parents would be advised to introduce present knowledge and all aspects of the youth's environment to him through the process of

---

[2] Jerome S. Bruner, *The Process of Education* (Cambridge: Harvard University Press, 1960) p. 20; *Strengthening Science Teaching in Elementary Schools,* Illinois Curriculum Program, bulletin No. C-Three, 1960, p. 27.

discovery. He should be allowed to participate, to choose, to search, sometimes to launch out alone, and, above all, to have the emotional rewards of his own personal discovery or invention just as the original discoverer or inventor had. Greater interest, sustained study, and significant increments of learning result when a fact or a principle is discovered through the young person's pursuit of his own question. Giving answers is no spur to learning. Giving the young learner an opportunity to "look it up" or experiment for himself, and then asking him further questions relevant to his search so as to stimulate his curiosity to know more and grasp relationships — these are magic spurs to learning.

No one will deny that young people need an effective and usable knowledge of subject matter. The method of discovery highlights the way in which the learner acquires subject matter. It is concerned also with the attitudes the young explorer is developing in the process of learning. On this point, Jerome Bruner of Harvard University thinks the critical attitudes to be developed through the method of discovery are:

1. Open-minded inquiry
2. Intellectual courage for shrewd guessing and hunches
3. Self-reliance in learning to solve problems on one's own
4. Conviction that nature and the universe has order one can and should discover.

Bruner thinks, further, that these attitudes have to be "caught" from teachers and parents who exemplify them in their own activity. Such teachers do not teach by assertion and demonstrated proof; instead, they inject an element of excitement into the discovery situation that entices the young person to discover ideas and relationships with some of the same joy and exciting sequences of the first scientist or scholar who traveled that path.[3] This is not to say that an intelligent teacher will not occasionally resort to systematic and deductive coverage of topics which may fill in gaps or follow a series of inductive enterprises. The important thing to remember is that the over-all process should be one of discovery; however, discovery should not be used to the frustration level.

By contrast, schools which emphasize memorizing cold content through verbalizing experiences of others tend to develop in children the habits of uncritical acceptance, of dependence on the opinions of others, and of dogmatism. It is a sad picture when children constantly

---

3 Bruner, *op. cit.*, pp. 20-21.

turn to the teacher or to the textbook for approved answers. Every young person needs aid in making mature responses in terms of his readiness, but this is not accomplished by "spoon feeding."

To develop intellectual self-reliance and to spur the zest for intellectual pursuit is not to give answers but to pose questions. This involves capitalizing upon, or creating, problem situations in which interesting questions arise.[4] Children are fascinated by the call of the unknown especially when a stimulating person issues the call. The enthusiasm of a teacher or a parent is contagious. Whether organized learning activities in a group convey children on a voyage of discovery or whether the individual "looks it up" at home, the same atmosphere can prevail. That atmosphere can be provided by either the teacher or the parent. Both can manage the environment so that the child's excitement about learning can be reinforced rather than ignored or discounted. Both can see that essential materials and references are available so that unnecessary frustration does not develop. Since children do not always know how or what to learn in order to solve their problems, frustration may occur if the parent or the teacher is not alert to the technical difficulties faced by children in their quests. Outside interference and too much domination of the process can dull the zest for pursuit, but parents and teachers can, nevertheless, open many doors to new learning when a moment of readiness arrives.[5]

Experiments and things to do

The YOUNG PEOPLE'S SCIENCE ENCYCLOPEDIA does not limit its presentation to information in articles, definitions, and cross references. To be sure, many interesting questions are posed in the main text of the encyclopedia. Included with many of the main articles, however, are special experiments and things to do. These are set off in a page column near the textual material in order to highlight them for easy reference. Arranged as they are in a separate "box" on the page, the more than 200 experiments and things to do can be used by the young person as if he had a separate book of experiments.

The technique of working out these experiments and things to do is a more systematic adaptation of the method of discovery. Each experiment or activity poses a question. One can find the answer only by doing the steps indicated. This is the way scientists verify their hypotheses or "hunches" about things in nature and the universe. Experimentation is a part of the scientific method and a necessary part of the job of the scientist.

---

[4] W. Ray Rucker, *Curriculum Development in the Elementary School* (New York: Harper & Brothers, 1960) p. 35.
[5] *Ibid.,* pp. 96-97.

Children have fun doing science experiments. They are like games and give added zest to learning. They teach them at the same time the discipline and order which must prevail in all scientific endeavor. Accuracy in measurement, in keeping records, and in reporting results becomes quite understandable to the child as a result of his attempts to experiment. Very often, in the beginning, the young person will fail in performing the experiment correctly because he did not take seriously enough the instructions to be exact. When he learns to be careful and accurate, his joy in performing experiments increases. The rewards are even greater. Therefore, experimenting may seem at first just like a game, but the child soon learns it is not the same as play. It can, fortunately, be more fun than play.

One concept the young person will learn early in experimenting is the concept of "control." A control in experimentation simply means that the experiment is in two parts. Not all experiments have two parts or a control, but many do, particularly when the experimenter wants to see if the new conditions to be tested are different from usual conditions. Thus, the control is the ordinary or usual way of doing things. The experimental situation has the new or different ingredients. When the experiment is concluded, the two situations are compared to see what different results occurred. If results are significantly different, the scientist may infer that the new ingredients or factors in the experimental situation were responsible for the difference.

The materials to be used in the experiments suggested in this encyclopedia are rather simple and are easy to obtain in most communities. It is important that all necessary materials are available before the experiment is attempted.

Developing critical and intuitive thinking

Critical thinking is valuable to both science and the everyday social process: Its chief characteristic probably is that it can recognize assertions lacking in substance or proof. The critical thinker is quick to recognize faults in thinking. He uses a systematic way of determining if something is true, reliable, or workable. Critical thinking is a form of scientific method or reflective thinking which ordinarily goes through, even if very quickly, these progressive steps:

1. Recognition of a problem or a question
2. Analysis of the problem, plans of attack, and the general search for information or data
3. Development of hypotheses and structure of further search for information in terms of them

4. Selection of the best solution and testing it by experimentation
5. Development of a tentative conclusion
6. Further verification of conclusions and reporting of findings to others.

Since the critical thinker is trained in thinking like the scientist, scholar, or philosopher, he realizes that even under the most controlled conditions the human mind is able to find only a *best* answer, not necessarily *the* answer. Many good answers have had to give way to others as science and technology advance. Science searches for the truth, but the quest is never ended. One can never be sure he has found the ultimate truth. The critical thinker is skeptical, therefore, when he hears others claim an indisputable truth, of having all factors under control, or of perfecting a cure-all.

The critical thinker looks also for cause and effect relationships. He wants to look beyond the symptoms of a situation, beyond even the ways in which the symptoms are affecting behavior, to the cause of the symptoms. He is more confident that a reliable solution can be worked out for problems if analysis goes down to the bedrock of cause.

If someone wants to launch out on a new enterprise with little except enthusiasm, the critical thinker is there to ask, "What are your plans?" He does not believe that things will "naturally work themselves out." He wants coordination, schedules, intermediate goals, organization of resources, and the like before he can give his approval of even the most worthy goals. He wants plans to be evolved through scientific thinking.

Intuitive thinking, on the other hand, sometimes appears to dispense with steps in definition and analysis with the related search of available data. It appears to leap immediately to a shrewd guess, to a tentative solution without the patient labor of the scientist. Although anyone may engage in intuitive thinking, it is most likely to appear in the individual with a particularly acute creative imagination. Some of the most valuable products of intuitive thinking come from advanced scholars and mature scientists whose knowledge has reached such a high state of generalization they can reach conclusions about unknowns in their own and related fields of knowledge by using the generalizations previously reached. In other words, they see *transfer* value between the familiar and the unknown. Their "hunches" often pay off because phenomena do tend to act in terms of certain broad laws. If enough of the structure or the specifics of a known situation seem to be present in the unknown situation, the creative imagination of the intuitive thinker constructs the new situation partly with the image he has already constructed of the related situation.

The chief value of intuitive thinking is that it gives us problems-with-tentative-solutions-to-be-tested. Great intuitive thinkers are the scouts of science. They forge ahead to explore what the main body of scientists should explore more systematically. Thus, intuitive thinking should be checked carefully by the above steps which characterize scientific thinking. It may result in important short cuts in the progress of science, but there is no substitute for the rigorous testing by the scientific method.

Intuitive thinking has a place in the classroom and in the parent-child discussion. The young person needs to have courage and confidence in his ability to use intuitive thinking effectively. Children who lack such confidence probably should not be encouraged to use this type of thinking initially. With most above-average and gifted youngsters, the technique can be successfully nurtured. One effective way to teach intuitive thinking is, again, by example. If teachers or parents are willing to make the best guess about an answer and then encourage young persons to join them in critical analysis to test the guess, they are more likely to encourage this kind of courage on the part of the young. Obviously, training in intuitive thinking is impossible if the adult analyzes everything in advance. The analysis comes in the discovery process when the intuitive thinker and his associates set about to "discover if I am right."

The YOUNG PEOPLE'S SCIENCE ENCYCLOPEDIA presents an excellent opportunity for the adult and the young person to engage deliberately in intuitive thinking. Suppose a generalization or scientific principle had been learned in one volume of the encyclopedia. The young person may be encouraged to think where this principle might apply elsewhere. Following up the hunches may take both on a profitable voyage of discovery in several volumes. One of the best clues to relationships to other concepts, and thus to related generalizations, is the cross reference. Cross references are marked in small capital letters in the text of articles, and at the end of articles they are indicated by "See Also:".

An example of this kind of intuitive thinking and its implications for a systematic search for proof in the encyclopedia may be seen in a young person's hunch that the force of gravity is different on each of the planets, and different on the moon from that of Earth. This leap in intuitive thinking is not a great one for an adult. For a nine-year-old child it is a substantial leap. Perhaps it was occasioned by the child's reading elementary books on space and space travel in which the reader was informed that man will weigh less on the moon than on Earth, but that if man travels to Jupiter he will weigh much more. Part of the leap in the child's thinking is made by relating weight with the force of gravity. Part of it can be accounted for in the knowledge the child has about the different sizes of the planets and the size of the moon in relation to the earth. With these relationships, the child now leaps to his hypothesis that greater size and greater force of gravity go together in the solar system. Is his guess right? It is not exactly right, but his guess will lead to a refined answer if he is encouraged to follow up his guess with systematic search of proof in the encyclopedia.

To check his guess, the young intuitive thinker may read the article on "gravity" and follow up the indicated cross references. He should be encouraged next to study more closely the characteristics of the planets and of the moon. The guiding adult may pose the questions at this point: "Are all planets composed of the same material? Does a cube of this material weigh the same on all planets? Do any planets have very light material like that of a comet?" This analysis will lead the young person to realize that size alone may not account for the differences in the force of gravitation among the planets. He will discover that the density of their matter, or the total weight of the material in the planet, has a more exact relationship with the force of gravitation on objects on or near the planetary surface.

The kind of systematic analysis and search for proof by the young person may prepare him for another intuitive leap. He has been studying about members of the solar system. His attention should be directed to the sun and its immense size and weight. Its gravitational pull on the planets keep them from flying off into space in haphazard fashion. But why does not this great attraction pull the planets into the sun itself? If the youngster has encountered the idea of regular orbits for each planet as they revolve around the sun, he is ready for his leap to a new relationship. He sees the planets arranged in a great wheel around the sun which acts as the hub. The planets move around at different speeds, but there is *order* in this difference because their speed of travel around the sun is closely related to their distance from the sun. The closest planet, Mercury, moves fastest in the shortest orbit. Venus is second in distance from the sun; it moves slower in a longer orbit. This is true of each planet in turn. Perhaps our young reader has also encountered the idea that the solar system is a part of another and greater revolving system, the Milky Way Galaxy. His intuitive hunch, then, is that *order* in the universe of heavenly bodies is based on the balance of gravitational force and the speed of revolution. As he reads about man-made satellites, he will see the connection between their speeds and their distances from the earth's surface. A satellite can be placed successfully in orbit only if the rocket which takes it aloft attains the exact speed of revolution to balance the gravitational pull of the earth. Our young reader can check his guess, in part, by referring to the article on "satellite, man-made." If he wishes to persist in this study, he may be guided to the article on "motion."

Critical and intuitive thinking should be thought of as partners in the pursuit of the unknown. Both will be employed in any skillful use of this encyclopedia. The experiments and things to do throughout the first 19 volumes are planned to give the young person a systematic approach to critical or scientific thinking. Training in intuitive thinking depends upon the teachers and parents who guide young people in the use of the set.

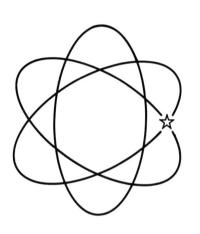

Index

HOW TO USE THIS INDEX
KINDS OF ENTRIES

Major entries are in bold print: **WEATHER**
Minor entries are in regular print: Agouti
Related entries are in italics: *Weather forecasting*

ABBREVIATIONS

Pictures are indicated by *illus.*
Experiments and Things to Do are indicated by *exp.*

NUMBERING

The *volume* number is given first, followed by
a *colon* and the *page* numbers: 2:153-155

INDEX OF THINGS TO DO